Jaded

Owen Patterson

BREVIS Publishing ■ Chicago

Sweet dreams interrupted
World ablaze

Harsh realities
Sobering

Jaded and broken

Blood red twilight
Streets filled with
Glistening shards
Glass bits and embers

I bide time 'till

The next crash
The next fire

        Jaded and Broken

Titles by Owen Patterson

The Dis-condition of Ease (prose fiction, 2015)

Lovely Faze (poetry, 2017)

Stars at Naught (poetry, 2018)

Jaded (poetry, 2018)

Fear Naught
The Junk Drawer of Poetry (poetry/prose, 2019)

See online book reviews at *Windy City Reviews*

Copyright © 2018 by Owen Patterson

All rights reserved. No part of this book may be used or reproduced in any manner whatsoever without the written permission of the Author/Publisher.

BREVIS Publishing, Chicago, IL USA 2018 **EDIT x7.1**
ISBN: 978-0-9964834-5-2 (BREVIS), 978-1720978572 (CS)

Formatting by Owen Patterson
Cover design by "Pica"; Edmund Barca
Editing by Gallus "Giblet" Morsél

Special Thanks:
Yasmeen Patterson Ahmad, Edmund Barca Gaylord, Gallus Morsél, Danyal Kim

Thanks for your advice and help.

A pure light
A gift from God

Even standing in shadow
Illuminates

Light unshielded
Obliterates malevolence

The unprepared
Rendered blind

The ready see
For eons' eons

> *Gifted Light Pure*
> *for Karin Janine*

CONTENTS

DESCRIPTION (Poem) *Jaded and Broken*
CREDITS
DEDICATION (Poem) *Gifted Light Pure*
INTRO (Poem) *Tree Falling*

1 ■ *Arc* (Poem) *How I Am*
Through Space (1), Ever Behold Thee (3),
Swept Away (5), Beautiful Eyes (7),
Thinking of You While Sobering (9),
If Only To Be Blissful (11), Alarm Bell Timbre (13)

2 ■ *Subject Impermanence* (Poem) *The Dynamic*
Observer's Tell (17), Cerulean Globes (19),
Non Grata (21-22), Endure This Day (25),
Rampart Devil (27), The Light For Last (29),
Rapid Detox (31), Dandelion (33)

3 ■ *Tethers* (Poem) *Echo*
A Stifling Sound (37), Semantics and Propaganda (39),
Mired In Echo (41), The Last Man's Overture (43-44),
Juxtaposed (47), They (49)

4 ■ *Startled Awake* (Poem) *Silver In Glass*
Razor Wire and Barbs (53), The Little Girl Suffers (55),
Mother's Day (57-58), Blessed (61-62),
Ashes To Ashes (65)

5 ■ *Real-ish* (Poem) *I Sweat A Lot*
Real-ish (69), Ambo-eye-dixtroyrity (71-72),
Dear D'Elise (75), Rhythm Soul Spirit House (77-78),
47th and Chill (81), Catalogue Poem (83-84),
What Rhymes With Nuggets? (87),
Whah-hah-hah-hah-haaah (89), Happy Cat (91)

CONTENTS

6 ■ *Shuck and Jive* ...*Does this make any sense?*
Ode To Little Billy Bobby (95-96), Oder Boy (99),
D.D.D. (101), One Felon Be Less (103)

7 ■ *Breathe Exhale* ...*Complex matter metabolized*
I Sparrow Fly Wide (107), Ver, Verde, Verdad (109),
Sound (111), Not By The Poet's Mind (113)

8 ■ *Logic and Magic* (Poem) *One's Choice*
Art (117), Between Logic and Magic (119),
The Abstract and The Natural (121),
Captured Heart (123), Desire (125)

9 ■ *Posts* (Poem) *Enjoy!*
Cinnamon (129), The Fight (131), She (133),
Repollo (135), Pegs (137), Context (139),
Impermanence (141), I love Your Cake (143),
Humans (145), Just Gone (147), That Glitch (149),
Give Good Things (151), Poetic License (153),
I Déja Vu'd Your Trappings (155),
Engender Perfection (157)

10 ■ *Coda* ...*The Challenge*
Uncivil Obedience (161), For Spite (163)

Gratitude

I have graduated
from simile to
metaphor

I *am* a tree
falling in the woods
when no one is around

Tree Falling

Arc

*Most people think,
therefore, they are.*

I feel, therefore, I am.

How I Am

Through Space

Hurling and tumbling
Feet not planted
Body not crashed
Frozen moments

The betweens are falling
Uncertain individuals
The fortunate finds another
With whom to journey

Ever Behold Thee

Of true words

Ever Beauty
In Beholder's eye

And Beholder to Beauty
Says truly
"Ever I... behold thee."

"What irony...
My beloved singular object,
2nd person pronoun,
cares not for poetry."

Swept Away

The jade
It did not break

While...
Her necklace

Break...

Bone
Tendon
Muscle
Blood, red flow

Debris field remains
Waste
Stained glass
Strewn
Shards in situ
Glisten with sunset
Masterful
Masterpiece
A lifetime
A mosaic composition

Upon completion
The mandala swept away

Beautiful Eyes

Flashback

Beautiful Eyes
Calm me down
Beautiful Eyes
Turn 'round
Don't walk 'way
Stay, with me
Never leave
I, what you need
You, what I need
Life, be a tree
We, be a seed
Future, be the fruit
And love, be the truth

Beautiful Eyes
Turn 'round
Don't walk 'way
Stay
Calm me down

Thinking of You While Sobering Haikus 1 and 2

I breathe deep, close eyes
Dreaming of still waterfalls
See you there, I cry

Blood red rivers flow
O'er brown Amazon jungle
New Doc fix with stitch

If Only To Be Blissful

Blissful
And ignorant

Never to remember
Lover's tender

If only, to forget
Woman's kiss
Heart's grip
We remiss

But what joy
To not know

Memory's an illusion

If only, to neglect
And not regret

What joyous thoughts
Precede the sorrow
That follows loss

Alarm Bell Timbre
(Kərsəd Cindered Remains)

Oh… how Cindered
Dreams away

Any fare rendered
For guaranteed sway

Tender pressed lips
Smoldering first kiss

Unhindered by
The chill fall morn

'Till cursed alarm bell timbre
Oh… how Cindered remains

Longing and forlorn

2

Subject Impermanence

Groupthink
Herd mentality
The family mob

Conform!
Conform!
Conform!

Clique
Or cast away

    The Dynamic

Observer's Tell

Art provocateur
Alluring palette
Abstract unveils
Reveals innermost
Unwitting confessions
In gallery sessions

Cerulean Globes

Fine Christian lady

Fine liberal heathen

Ne're nethers enchant
And loin's lonesome endurance
A member's companion not found
Leaves frustrated
Globes o' cerulean blue

Non Grata

Object permanence
Does not endure
Matures to
Selective
Subjective
The truly impermanent

Creative percepts
Devolve adept

Abate fondness
The consequence

Neither mind
Nor sense
Simply out of sight

He does not choose to be
Of many felled trees
Unheard and unseen

Graduates he
State abating
Simile
Dislike rendered

Metaphored
Sundered
And abhorred

Not simply unseen
Not *like* unwant
Non Grata
His presence affronts

Endure This Day

He dreamt yesternight
Of love and grace
So intensely bright
Lo, he covered his face

Petition unheard
Paid no price
Crows third
Once, twice, thrice

Seek grace
For he has none
Divination of fate
For all is done

Fall passed
Winter approach
Cold winds blast
He has no cloak

If this be the time
Then he need know
Give the sign
And he shall go

Endure this day
For love and grace
Come what may
Reveals his face

Rampart Devil

Devil at the rampart... thou shalt not breach!

Concern thee not with stone walls
Neither with crenels nor merlons
But with arrows to pierce thy mail
Stones thrown to break thy ranks and bones
And tar to burn thy flesh!

Devil, mine heart not to breach!

The Light For Last

You're a shark
And I'm swimming
Blood water dark
Eyes dimming

Turn my back
See the sun
Then you attack
'Till it's done

Nothing's left
You've won
You were best
I am gone

Last bit of light
In my eyes
Last bit of fight
Never again I rise

Rapid Detox

Internal flux
Massive drops
Of rapid detox

OK...
So...
Brain chemistry changed

Range of state
State of mind
Her smile
Gets me high

OK...
So...
The apple
And the eye
Intoxicate

Then... goodbye
Cannot debate
Cannot deny
Brain chemistry changed

Absent her smile
Kills my high

Internal flux
Massive drops
Of rapid detox

OK

Dandelion

On high set
Rose in pot or kettle
How you forget
Others do show mettle

Understanding scarce
Yet, words advance
Superlative fare
Expressive romance

You suggest, nevertheless
A dandelion to be
A rose, in jest
Can you not see?

By any other name
Romanticized
A rose just the same
In time will die

I do not, truly
Understand your intent
Denying beauty
Time, not well spent

Tethers

I speak, as Father spoke.
I write, as Mother wrote.
I live and I die. We are echo.

Echo

A Stifling Sound

Hold us down
Movement of money
The only sound
World suffering
Given gifts
Petty, conditional, insufficient
Provide not buffering
But hold us down
This popular philosophical thought abounds
And the misdirectional gibberish noise
A stifling sound

Semantics and Propaganda

All men equal
We the people
Propaganda
Taxation
Semantic
Representation
All equal
All people
Save for
Slaves or
Natives and
Lost lands and
Independence Day!
So say... the founders
How is their constitution?

Census
Tax us
Make sense of
Taxation... with
Representation
Expat... Brit
Count one man
African slave... save
Not more than
Three fifths... and
Tax the Native Man
Not at all... and
All not equal
All not people
All semantics and propaganda

Mired In Echo

I'm sorry
I only heard the echo
Library depository
Grassy knoll
It is no… thing
It is echo

Ropes in trees
Tethers, boats, and seas
Sounds so real
I am mired in it

So preach!

"I have a rapid eye movement!
Pettus and pavement
No fret
No shame
Little Selmas and little Lorrains
Lunch counters and board games
Play hand in hand
Sing and dance"

This kingdom
We build
Yet, Camelot killed
And King felled
By echoes

Ropes in trees
Tethers and boats and seas

It is so real
That we are mired in it

The Last Man's Overture

Men with brand of sin
Nothing is absolute
As was told
I dispute
What they hold as truth

Those with *White* robes
Have often said:

"Hell burns hot
On the outer edge of Heaven
Look in
Enter not
Ye men
With mark of sin
From end at begin
Hellfire burns
Burned you
Outside within
As *We* have written"

Men with branded skin
Yours is virtue
Not sin
Nothing is absolute
As was told
I dispute
What they hold as truth

Those with *White* robes
Have fear

Enlist your instrument
Strike the chord
Swift and expedient
Lift your sword
Join in
The Last Man's Overture

The first shall be last
And the last shall be first
We have lived last
But are not cursed
From end at begin
Heaven we've earned
Earned you
Outside within

We are first!

We are first!

Juxtaposed

Suffering… juxtaposed
Suppose
Strife
Fleeting life
Rife, with impermanence
Discernment, of greater distance
Existence
Follow signs
Hind sighted enlightenment
Juxtaposed
Suppose

Life fleeting

Strife

They

From this world they flee
Looking for a peaceful ecstasy

Their life is a search
One to the sea

Despair, the find
A violent anxiety

Face they to the wind
Some to their graves
They the wind sends

Startled Awake

Shinny glass distortion
Malfunction

Tap a prostitute on the shoulder

The rich see opportunity
The wise have insight
The rebel finds a rebel making
A mother loves a child

Silver In Glass

Razor Wire and Barbs

Sweaters unravel
Cold gathers
Thread drawn through razor wire
Love exposed in lands occupied
Blockades, walls, fences, and barbs
Stones thrown against bulldozers
Tanks thrown against homes and memories
Desperate children that know only war
And a world without empathy

The Little Girl Suffers

Why does the little girl suffer
Why does she beg
Deep water, she went under
Tears like lead

Mother can't help no more
Powers don't care
Burdened chains of poor
An' my wallet's bare

I see the little girl suffer
Why does she beg
No life preserver
She's just dead

Mother's Day

A young woman's dream
Shrieks and screams
Haunting details of a
Haunting boy
Who failed...
To stop

Just kept swimming
She adrift
Head spinning
Creatures thrusting
Water churning
Shadows twisting
A soul is turning
And will not stop

The poor woman
Has gone aground
And hit a rock

Startled awake
A breath to take
She hails her first
With the urgency of birth
Sitting up in her linen sea
Dizzy, confused, and hurt

She knows that what is
Was not
She knows
That he did not stop
He just kept swimming

Blessed

I am not different
But I did not rape the tree
As did she
The one whom I love
And detest equally

She did my desire
She did what I could not
For I am a coward
She spoke to the serpent
And caressed his fire

I admire them all
In no certain order
Nanny, sister, and daughter
Wife, mother, and lover

I, about myself, almost forgot
That I would have
Had she not
I would have raped the tree
As did she
The one whom I love
And detest equally

We were given love
We stole knowledge
And we learned hate
And indifference

In her
Lies true strength, ambition
And timely tenderness

If we survive the serpent's hex
Then she is not cursed
But truly Blessed

Ashes To Ashes

Life ends
Death begins
A corpse life goes forever
Simple stillness
Inevitable decay
From ashes we came
Of ashes we stay

In dirt children play
Before fated days
Dirt, where they root
Where they grow
From ashes we came
To ashes we go

Real-ish

On hot and humid days,
I am fond of telling people that
my father was a stick of butter...
and my mother was a biscuit.

Don't think too much about it.

I Sweat A Lot

Real-ish

Not gibber*ish*
Not gibber*shit*
Not nonsense
Not non-*ish*
This's real-*ish*

Ambo-eye-dixtroyrity

Ambo-eye-dixtroyrity
Pretty mamma why you lie to me
Pretty mamma
Dissin' be a buggin' me
Say ambo-eye-dixtroyrity

Saw you wash one hand
With the other
An' the other with the other
Good God!
What a lubba

High an' low
Below an' a bub
I got addition
Seriously, a diction
To yor lub

I rea-cogg-ano-nice you
An' you rea-cogg-ano-nice me
I'm hypo-therma-nice singin' blue
'Bout enflame heart py-rastit-ity
Got it bad fo you
An' you ain't got chit fo me

Oh well
Hell's bells
My head swells
'Cause it fit
Like a glub
Got addition
Seriously, a diction
To yor lub

You wishin' in da washin'
Like a sage
Yor in-diss-incision
Like new-clear dissin'fission
Is caustin' me my age

Not you ain't good in da wash
An' I certainly be wishin'
But please make dat diss-incision
I'll be missin'
Yor lub

Good God!

What a lubba

Dear D'Elise

Dear D'Elise
Oh Dear D'Elise
Where have you been
Been weeks and weeks
Oh Dear D'Elise
My good friend
My good friend

Dear D'Elise
Oh Dear D'Elise
Come right in
Got clean sheets
Oh Dear D'Elise
My how we sin
My, how we sin

Dear D'Elise
Oh Dear D'Elise
Your stature kills
My body's weak
Oh Dear D'Elise
Heart be still
Heart, be still

Dear D'Elise
Oh Dear D'Elise
Skin's so soft
Smile's so sweet
Oh Dear D'Elise
My love won't stop
My love, won't stop

Rhythm Soul Spirit House

Plays over
Rolls under
Rhythms fade
Motion
Melody
New rhythms made
Melancholy Babe
Step to the next faze
It's laid
Back in
Twist out
What's in my head
Is in my house

Plays over
Rolls under
Sound
Distant thunder
I wonder at
Not understand it
Not candid
How can it... be
The pause for my
Melancholy
The cause for my
Melancholy Baby

Step to the rhythm fade
It's laid
Back in
Twist out
What's in my head
Is in my house

Roll with it
Over under
Spirit get high
Shades to the face
Color glass to the sky
Step in pace
Step by and by
No look my face
No look my eye

Some things better
Left alone
This is my house
This is my home
Step to the next phase
Step to the laid
Back in
Twist out
What's in my head?

Rhythm Soul Spirit House

47th and Chill (Based on a real event)

ASS! ASS! ASS! ASS! ASS! (Ringtone)

"Yo! I'm at 47th Street; waitin' on the bus.
You gonna pick me up?
Well, you asked where I'm at.
So, I thought you was gonna pick me up.

You cookin' me somethin'?
Well, you asked if I was comin' over.
I thought you was gonna cook me somethin'.

Yeah, I'm coming' over.
Well, can we at least chill?
Ah'ight. Bet!"

Catalogue Poem

A Fri/End
A pot
Bro/Kin Hi/Coo
Memo/Reason
Thought
Not Remembered

There's nothing like a poet
Feels good
Inspired
Nothing to say
Ma and Pa Kettle music
Sounds good tonight
Homeboys enter seen
As clock strike 3
Talkin' shit
One to the other,
"I wanted coffee an' a burger,
an' you order me orange juice an' a Danish!"

w/Big Band soundtrack
Transmitted from the Ozone
Over the Bermuda Triangle
Pay the bill
Take a whiz
Time to go
Take the late train

Mo' homeboys
Talkin' shit,
"I picked her up at that last party.
She don't weigh but a hundred pounds."

"I'd buttfuck her 5,000 times!"

"She is fine, ain't she? But she ain't the kind
I'd marry."

Inspired verse?
Sure

Great poets?
Maybe

Inspired catalogue?
God

What Rhymes With Nuggets?
(My Brain Is Cheese)

Red line train
My brain
Is cheese
Please
Change the channel
I can't handle
I can't take
His music grates
My mouth pleads
The cheese bleeds
From the damage
I only manage
To say, "Taters later?"
He says, "What?"
I say, "What?"
He says, "What?"
I say...
"I prefer pō-tā-tō nuggets
What rhymes with nuggets?"

Lots of damnits and fuckits

Wah-hah-hah-hah-haaah

A Christian
That thinks he's a Jew
But believes in Karma

It could be nothing
He could be lost
He could be misunderstood
It could be…
The ramblings of a madman

Wah-hah-hah-hah-haaah

Happy Cat

I'm not crying for the past
Milk was spilled
The cat was there
It's taken care of
It's gone
I cry for what remains
The ridicule and mocking
Shameful
The happy sad irony
What milk does to a cat

Shuck and Jive

Does this make any sense?

Ode To Little Billy Bobby (Mental itty)

Does this make any sense?

Little Billy Bobby
Walked past the fence
The bomb
Commanded the wind to blow
Matter took an irregular flow
Billy Bobby's soul
Fell through a hole
A rip in space
Poor Billy Bobby
There was left no trace

No sense the fence
The bomb the blow
Irregular flow
Feelin' the ceilin'
On top of a rock
Mental nitty
Mental gritty

I don't understand
The mental itty

Was that a word I heard?
Shut up!
Don't gimme no flap
I can say what I want
'Cause this is my rap

I'll continue now

Here's little Billy Bobby
Floating through time
The rest of eternity
Thinking he's a lime
Traversing disconnected space
Using his feet to wash his face

This is certainly a shame
And we're all to blame

Little Billy Bobby
Floating through time
Thinking he's a lime
Disconnected space
Disconnected feet
Washin' his face

No sense the fence
The bomb the blow
Irregular flow
Feelin' the ceilin'
On top of a rock
Mental nitty
Mental gritty

I don't understand
The mental itty

Mentality

Of this so called
Civilized society

Order Boy

Hello
May I take your order?
You'll shuck and jive for a quarter
You'll lie cheat hustle
Use your pale pigmented muscle
Bitch for an inch
Push back me a mile
Then when I'm flustered overloaded runnin'
You flash that lazy contented ugly smile
And oooh nice watch
Contacts in your eyes
And oooh diamond ring
Cocaine to get you high
You lie cheat hustle
The order boy you press
Use your pale pigment muscle
Girlfriend to impress
And out in your Porsche
Oooh super nice car
But my dead-end job won't get *me* that far
And you wonder why *I'm* hostile
As you throw *your* fit
While just three generations ago
I was eatin' your shit
How quick you forget
So get out of my face
Leave this place
I hope you choke on your wealth
And if you don't like my poetry

Asshole!

Go order your food somewhere else

D. D. D. (AlliterateD)

OK
Ditty this
About Rich Dinero
Diamond Dick Dinero
Do not mistake
Diamond Dick... a diamond dick

Diamond Dick
The diamond dealer
In Detroit

Diamonds delineate dollars
Dogs do not distress
Dastardly deeds
Diamond Dick deals death
Dilettante dress
Diamonds desired
Downtrodden dig dirt
Do not mistake
Diamond Dick
Diamond dealer

Rich dick Dinero

One Felon Be Less

You're **H**onor
You are **J**udge
You are **J**ury
You are **E**xecutioner
Office of Peace
Fear the lot
Fear the not
Fear *is* justification
Fear *is* due process
Fear the felon progress
Fear the felon aggress
Office, have fearless
Fear *is* due process
One felon be resist
Do you're **D**uty!
Bullets egress
Civil regress
Civil oppress
Do you're **D**uty!
One felon be less

"Let God sort 'em out."

Breathe Exhale

Complex matter metabolized
Lungs expand, exchange, and expel
Neurons fire and interpret

I Sparrow Fly Wide

Arrow
Flies straight
Length of narrow

Not I
I sparrow
Fly wide
Every which way
Every which day

I breathe sorrow
And exhale joy

Ver, Verde, Verdad

Green
Interesting

Some would persuade
The color of envy
To be
The color of jade

Others do not suggest
But verily attest
With certainty
With veracity
Surety
As sky is blue
Jade to be
The color of truth

Sound

Cause and Effect through Sound

The Universe vibrates
Life and motion
Hearts beating
Life's blood coursing
Complex matter metabolized
Lungs expand, exchange, and expel
Neurons fire and interpret
Subatomic pendulums swing
Charges hold and release
And hold again
The Universe described
As radar paints

Vibes bounce
Interact and cause effect
No space empty
Energy teems and courses

The Body Cosmos
Roars and moans
Crackles and pops

Cause and Effect through Sound

Brilliant!

Not By The Poet's Mind

Poetic mind
Spins and bends
Waxy light
End to end
Inspired yearning
Twisted turning
Candles burn and burn

Drowsy calls
And achy falls
A damaged soul
The poet does know

Alludes does sleep
And sleep does elude
And sleep does choose
Its own time

Not by the poet's mind

Logic and Magic

Money or Love?

*A poor man of good character
will choose to love another.*

*A rich man of good character
will choose to love another.*

*A man of poor character...
will always choose to love himself;
never another.*

One's Choice

Oh, how art does analyses the observer

Art, the provocateur…

What comes forth?

Observers' unwitting confessions…

Art

Logic does not often explain matters of the heart.
The joy when I see my friend smile...
The sorrow that follows her absence...
Magic does not attempt to explain.
Magic merely acknowledges phenomena.
Between Logic and Magic

The Abstract and The Natural

Sundial
Tracking the path
Fire across the sky

I track shadows across her face
Illuminating questions of origin
Tackling fleeting concepts
With stick and disc
Seemingly elusive as
Asking a mama rhino
What's on her mind
The sundial yields few answers
The mama rhino answers decisively
"Get away from my baby!"

Beauty draws the eye

Character captures the heart

Captured Heart

Lust is desire

Love is desire that endures

Desire

Posts

Don't miss the awe and wonder of the show, while busy trying to debunk the magician.

Enjoy!

His and hers...

Crazy is like cinnamon
Too much ruins the pie

Whatever comes, will come.
In strong winds
the banner clings to the pole.
Both may topple.
There, in the fight, is found hope.

The Fight

I very much like women.
If God created us in His image,
I would imagine that
He, is a She.

She

When I hear the word
"repollo"
in my head it's
"Aw Ma... chicken again? I want
cabbage!"

Repollo

A square peg
that does not fit into a round hole
is not inherently wrong.
It is merely different.

One verse does not a book make

Context

If we live forever,
there would be no urgency
to achieve anything.

Impermanence defines our
earthly existence.

I love your intelligence,
kindness, conviction.
I love your good humor.
Your smile
is icing on the cake.

I Love Your Cake

Humanity
would be awesome

if not for the
Humans

I walked away.
I didn't want to tell the truth
and I didn't want to lie.

Just Gone

I dreamt that I had died.
I was cut to pieces and put into a box,
but I re-animated due to a glitch.
I saw my dad.
I told him I didn't want to die.
He said nothing and walked away.
I understood him;
that he loves me,
but couldn't save me.
I'm on a long march back to that box.
Re-animation was painful.
Death seemed easier.
Life is hard.
I don't know a lot,
but I'm going to work to fix that glitch.

Throughout our lives
we hear our parents' voices
in our minds.

Give your children
good things to remember.

Poetic license should extend to the reader.
The engaged observer creates through interpretation.
That individuals relate differently to a work of art
denotes its universality.

Difference does not have to be divisive.
Difference can be, unifying.

I Déjà Vu'd Your Trappings
(A response to Danyal Kim's "Korean Trash")

I read your piece
I opened my fridge
I decided I was Korean

Trappings...
We all got 'em

Perfection is in the effort,
not the result. Do the work.
Be genuine.

Engender Perfection

Coda

The Challenge...
Finding Light, In The Dark

Uncivil Obedience

Dark sky
Deplorable omens
Assault
Uncivil obediences
Not only one word presages
Empire's fall
Portent day's birth
Jaded

Prophesy Trumpet sounds end

The Meek Shall Inherit Earth

The Bold Destroy It

For Spite

Thank you for reading Jaded.

Look for a new title in 2019.

Sincerely,

Owen Patterson

www.ingramcontent.com/pod-product-compliance
Lightning Source LLC
Chambersburg PA
CBHW061646040426
42446CB00010B/1613